# THE POWER OF QUESTIONS
How to Use Intelligent Questions to Achieve Success with Friends, Family, Acquaintances and Yourself

## SCOTT RICHARDS

© **Copyright 2013 by Empowerment Nation - All rights reserved.**

This publication is designed to provide accurate and authoritative information in regard to the subject matter covered. It is sold with the understanding that the publisher is not engaged in rendering legal, accounting or other professional services. If legal advice or other professional assistance is required, the services of a competent professional person should be sought.

- From a Declaration of Principles jointly adopted by a Committee of the American Bar Association and a Committee of Publishers and Associations.

All rights reserved. No part of this publication may be reproduced or transmitted in any form or by any means, electronic or mechanical, including photocopy, recording, or any information storage or retrieval system, without permission in writing from the publisher.

No responsibility or liability is assumed by the Publisher for any injury, damage or financial loss sustained to persons or property from the use of this information, personal or otherwise, either directly or indirectly. While every effort has been made to ensure reliability and accuracy of the information within, all liability, negligence or otherwise, from any use, misuse or abuse of the operation of any methods, strategies, instructions or ideas contained in the material herein, is the sole responsibility of the reader.

Any copyrights not held by publisher are owned by their respective authors.

All information is generalized, presented for informational purposes only and presented "as is" without warranty or guarantee of any kind.

All trademarks and brands referred to in this book are for illustrative purposes only, are the property of their respective owners and not affiliated with this publication in any way. Any trademarks are being used without permission, and the publication of the trademark is not authorized by, associated with or sponsored by the trademark owner.

www.EmpowermentNation.com

## Table of Contents

Why Do We Ask Questions? ... 1
    Defining Objectives ... 5
    Three Reasons Questions are Asked ... 7
How are Questions Used? ... 11
    Comprehensive Assessment ... 11
    Who Questions ... 12
    What Questions ... 13
    Where Questions ... 15
    When Questions ... 16
    Why Questions ... 18
    How Questions ... 19
    Would Questions ... 20
    Affective Assessment ... 22
    Psychomotor Assessment ... 22
    Why Closed-Ended Questions Matter ... 23
Simple Rules for Communication ... 25
    Direct, Concise, and Simple ... 25
    Focus and Intent ... 27
    W.A.I.T. = Why Am I Talking? ... 28
    Know What to Do with the Answer ... 31
Communication in the Workplace ... 32
    The Questions of the Job Interview ... 32
    Employer-Employee Relationships ... 40
    Employee-Employee Relationships ... 42

The Questions of the Sales Pitch _____ 45
Choosing the Right Mode of Communication is Key! _____ 53
- Snail Mail _____ 53
- Email _____ 56
- Telephone _____ 59
- Scanners and Faxes _____ 62
- Internet Chat and Text Messaging ____ 62
- Video Chat _____ 63
- Social Media _____ 63
- Questions to Ask Yourself Before Communicating _____ 67

Communication with Friends and Family __ 70
- Family, Friends, Acquaintances, and Dates – Who are they and why do Questions Matter within these Relationships _____ 71
- The Family Unit – Communicating with Your Spouse and Children _____ 72
- Siblings, Parents, and Extended Family – Creating a Supportive Foundation with Questions _____ 77
- Friends and Acquaintances – What's to Ask? _____ 78
- Questions to Consider for Friends, Family, Acquaintances, and Dates _____ 80

Communicating in a Modern World: Connecting

with Friends, Family, and Love Interests via the Internet ----- 83
    To Friend or Not to Friend? Online Communication with Friends and How to Navigate Your Way through Social Media ----- 83
    Online Dating – Segue to Sex, or Meeting Mister Right? ----- 88
    Making the First Move: What Questions Do I Ask? ----- 90
Self Communication – Asking the Hard Questions ----- 93
    Determining Your Short-Term and Long-Term Objectives ----- 93
Conclusion ----- 97
    More Questions to Consider ----- 98

# Why Do We Ask Questions?

Most of our lives, we never question *why* we do what we do unless there are extremely high stakes at hand. We ask questions and give answers in a flow of communication that simply isn't examined - and why should it be? Why should we stop to consider the underlying reasons we're asking our spouse "What's for dinner?" What's to consider about asking someone the time of day? I'll tell you.

The manner in which we ask questions makes a remarkable difference in how we communicate. And that is just the tip of the iceberg. How we communicate is, in essence, the greatest factor in our happiness, our success, and our relationships. Having the ability to communicate effectively means the difference between the top CEO of a leading corporation and the guy sleeping on a leaky air-mattress in a hovel in Queens. Having the ability to communicate effectively means the difference between the happily married entrepreneur and the angry, bitter checkout woman that you detested last week getting groceries.

Communication is the essence of life - or at least the life that we share on this planet with others. And let's face it - in order to achieve success in the workplace, at home, and socially -

we have to know how to communicate. Questions are at the heart of that. Learning how to ask the right questions at the right times can literally change everything in your life. It can change how people perceive you. It can take you from the person least likely to succeed to the person considered the most empathetic, charming, outgoing, articulate, intelligent, and powerful in the room.

We ask questions for a number of different reasons, just as we make statements for a number of different reasons. We may want to impress someone with our knowledge. We may want to sway someone to our side. We may want to sell someone something. We may want to seduce someone. We may want to threaten someone. All of these are reasons that questions are asked.

But of course, you're thinking, "No. I ask questions because I want answers to them. I'm not trying to manipulate people. I just want to know what's for dinner!" And I'll have to say: not really. Yes, you may want to know what's for dinner, but there are many different ways that you can find that answer without asking the question. You can look in the oven and see what's in there. You can discern by scent. Why do you ask? You're engaging in conversation. The simple phrase "What's for dinner?" can mean a million different things in a million different circumstances. Quite often, its meaning has nothing to do with what's for dinner. Quite often it means "How was your day?"

Now consider for a moment that you're the one in the kitchen cooking dinner. Your spouse comes home from a long day, hangs up his jacket, and asks you, "What's for dinner?" What is your reply? "Lasagna" - or whatever may be in the pot. And you go back to stirring. What if the question were: "What smells so good? What inspired you to in tonight's creation?" Would you be more inclined to keep talking? Here, the answer still deals with dinner, but it opens the doors to thoughts, feelings, and experiences to share.

Now consider that your son has just brought you his report card. He's flunked two classes - math and reading. You ask him, "What happened? Why didn't you study harder?" He stares at the floor, not answering. You push him further, "Why didn't you ask me for help?" Still, nothing.

Now step back and place yourself in a different situation. You're at work and you've spent the past month developing a detailed report for your boss. It's been maddening, and you're just glad the whole thing is over with. You turned it in yesterday and today he calls you into his office. "What is this? What have you been doing for the past month?" he asks you. How do you reply?

Going back to your son with the bad report card, let's say that instead of asking him about his performance in the past, your response is: "Wow. This isn't too great. What do we need to do in order for this to improve the next semester? Is there some way that I can help?" Given those questions, your son is more likely to respond. He's already upset because of the grades - because at the very least he knows you'll be disappointed in him. What if, instead of making him feel worse, you *open the doors to finding a solution*?

What if your boss instead called you in with that report and said "Well, I can see what you've done here and that's great. But what I'm really looking for is X, Y, and Z. Do you think that you could rework this to include that?" You're certainly going to be more willing to comply than you'd be if you just felt accused and thrown on the defensive.

The point is that by considering our questions - how we ask them, why we ask them, when we ask them - we can turn around almost any situation imaginable. Perhaps Eugene Ionesco said it best: "It is not the answer that enlightens, but the question."

Are you ready to embark on a journey into the depths of the psyche? Are you ready to start asking the right questions? Are you ready to begin living a successful and happy life? Then read on.

## Defining Objectives

What is an objective? ***It's what you want to attain.*** We use a lot of different words that mean the same thing. You might consider this to be a "mission," a "goal," a "driving force," or any number of things. For our purposes we'll keep things simple by using "objective." Your objective is the apple that you're reaching for up high in the tree.

I don't mean to scare you, but you have an objective with every person you interact with. That doesn't make you some kind of snaky, underhanded manipulator – it makes you exactly like everyone else. Objectives don't always have to serve *you* in an obvious way – your objective can be "I want to make her happy." Why? "Because I love her." Your objective can be anything from "I want him to tell me what the real problem is" to "I desperately need him to sign this contract today."

Each objective requires different approaches. If you want someone to "open up" to you, you ask them open-ended questions like "What are your thoughts on that?" If you need a yes or no answer and you need it immediately, you're wasting your time with open-ended questions. You need a "Yes" or a "No." Knowing what your objective is makes all the difference in the world. If you know what it is you need from this person, you're that much closer to knowing how to phrase your questions.

H. Jackson Brown, Jr. said, "Remember that everyone you meet is afraid of something, loves something, and has lost something." He couldn't be more right. We often forget that the people we're dealing with - be them our spouses, children, coworkers, or clients - are just as sensitive as us, just as passionate as us, and just as aware as us. They have irrational fears and rational ones. They have hidden desires and prominent ones. Questions - and knowing how to use them - can expose those fears and desires and give you both a deeper understanding of and connection with the individual and an understanding of how best to achieve your own objectives.

Ask yourself:

- "What do I want from this person?"
- "Why am I asking them a question?"
- "What is the objective?"

The answers to these questions will determine every step you will take next. But you must ask them, and you must answer them honestly.

**Three Reasons Questions are Asked**

Essentially there are three reasons we pose questions. These "reasons" are not to be confused with our objectives—although they ultimately build toward the objective. We ask questions because we need an answer to be obtained or we need the question to be posed. Sometimes, the question itself is more important than the answer—we see this all the time in the educational setting. Below, we'll look at the three main reasons for questions and why each is important in a particular circumstance.

**The answer is important.**

The first reason questions are asked is that the answer is important. This is what most people think of when they think "questions." Why do you ask questions?

Because you need answers! Sometimes – perhaps even *most* of the time – this is true. But not always…

**The question is important.**

*Sometimes,* the answer is less important than the question. In these cases, the question itself is a tool that helps to develop answers. A good question can kick our brain into gear, so to speak. Consider the Zen kōan: "What is the sound of one hand clapping?" The process of a kōan is to provoke doubt; through questioning, may one find the truth. The process of questioning firmly-held beliefs can open many new avenues of insight.

"A good question is never answered. It is not a bolt to be tightened into place but a seed to be planted and to bear more seed toward the hope of greening the landscape of idea."

--John Ciardi

**The process of asking is important.**

Why is the process of asking a question important? It shows that we care what the other person thinks, feels, and wants. Imagine for a moment that your spouse bursts into the living room to announce: "I just bought a new car!" What is your reaction? If this is an unexpected purchase, you might respond, "Why did you not discuss this with me first?" Now imagine how differently this scenario might progress if, instead of making grandiose announcements, you instead shared your desire to buy a new car with your spouse and asked, "What do you think about that?"

The process of asking questions indicates our willingness to share our objectives with others and to include their thoughts, feelings, and desires in our decision-making. A question like "What was the happiest day of your life?" shows that we're interested in knowing more about someone. Questions can be used to ensure trust, or they can be used to expose hidden agendas.

"A sudden bold and unexpected question

doth many times surprise a man and lay him open." – Francis Bacon

# **How are Questions Used?**

According to Bloom's Taxonomy, a classification of learning objectives within the educational system, there are three main "domains" of educational objectives: the cognitive, affective, and psychomotor domains. Cognitive domain skills relate to knowledge and critical thinking. Affective skills illustrate how an individual reacts emotionally to different stimuli, and psychomotor skills relate to an individual's ability to use tools. These domains play an important role in how we use questions.

**Comprehensive Assessment**

Comprehension questions include "who, what, when, where, why, and how" questions. These questions assess how well an individual understands a concept, but questions that include "who, what, when, where, why, and how" can have a number of different objectives. Consider each of the following questions and how they might apply in different situations. How could these questions be used to achieve different objectives?

**Who Questions**

We often imagine that questions beginning with "who" are focused on answers that require a named response. "Who was the first President of the United States?" In reality, though, "Who Questions" can lead to a great number of answers. "Who do you want to spend your life with?" This question doesn't necessarily require a named answer – it refers to the characteristics you want in the person you may potentially be with. "Who are you?" What does this question mean to you, beyond your simple name? Consider the following "Who Questions" and take in the myriad of answers that might come to mind. "Who Questions" are important because they examine the characteristics of people, including ourselves.

- Who am I?
- Who do you think is the best candidate for the job?
- Who are you? Who should lead us?
- Who should buy from us?
- Who needs our services?
- Who do I want to be?

- Who do you trust?
- Who is that?
- Who would you like to spend the rest of your life with?
- Who irritates you?
- Who do you think you are?
- Who asked you?
- Who should I ask?
- Who is the smartest?
- Who will help me succeed?
- Who do you love?
- Who are your heroes?

**What Questions**

"What" is a pronoun that can be used interrogatively as a request for specific information, to inquire about the character or occupation of a person, to inquire as to the origin, identity of something, to inquire as to the worth, usefulness, force, or importance of something, or to request a repetition of words or information not fully understood. "What" is a pretty all-encompassing word. Unlike "who," "what" is not relegated to humankind. "What" does not discriminate. Examine the following "What Questions" and consider your responses. Answering "What is the meaning of X to me?" is how we determine how X assimilates into our objectives and desires. "What is the meaning of life to you?" Here are more:

- What do I want?
- What am I going to do?
- What have I done?
- What do they want?
- What are they thinking?
- What should we do?
- What are your thoughts on that?
- What is important to you?
- What should I have done?
- What is your plan?
- What makes you happy?
- What kind of music do you like?
- What happened?

- What are your greatest fears?

- What is the thing you are proudest of in your life?

- What is the greatest obstacle you've overcome in your life?

- What do you wish there were more of in your life?

- What makes you respect a person?

- What have you learned from your experiences?

- What do you want to achieve?

- What would you like to know?


**Where Questions**

"Where Questions" can imply a specific location or they can refer to particular circumstances or even a "place in time." "Where do you want to be?" is a question that can be answered with a place or circumstances: "I want to be in a position that is respected" is one answer. "I want to be in Hawaii" is another. Consider the following "Where Questions" and their implications. "Where" might these questions come up?

- Where am I?
- Where have I been?
- Where am I going?
- Where should we go from here?
- Where did you grow up?
- Where do you want to live?
- Where are your favorite memories?
- Where do you consider home?
- Where would you like to grow old?
- Where did you study?
- Where do you go for fun?
- Where is the most beautiful place you've been?
- Where is a place you dislike?
- Where did you last see it?

**When Questions**

"When Questions" can refer to a specific

time or to specific circumstances. "When will you be home?" is a simple "When Question" that refers to time. "When are you happiest?" examines the circumstances that surround your happiness. You could respond "I am happiest when I am surrounded by friends and family" or you could respond "I am happiest in the morning." Consider the following "When Questions" and how they apply to your life:

- When were you born?

- When did you decide this?

- When are you going to do that?

- When was the happiest time in your life?

- When is the deadline?

- When did you choose your career?

- When did you meet?

- When will we see results?

- When did you discover your passions?

- When is the best time to reach you?

- When will you be ready?

- When will you be home?

- When are you happiest?

**Why Questions**

"Why" is the ultimate of questions. "Why" examines the reasoning behind matters. "Why" can follow almost any other question's response. "Why" generally means "for what reason," and therefore "Why Questions" often directly refer to our objectives. "Why did you do that?" is a question that examines the objectives of the actions of an individual. The answers to "Why Questions" will tell you the reasoning behind the individual being asked. "Why Questions" are also sometimes the hardest to answer. Consider these "Why Questions" and look deeply into your answers. It is in these answers that you will discover your innermost desires and your life objectives.

- Why am I here?
- Why do I want that?
- Why should I care?
- Why do you want that?
- Why do you think that?
- Why am I worried?

- Why does it matter?
- Why not?
- Why does he do that?
- Why not try this?
- Why did you do that?
- Why is it important?

**How Questions**

"How Questions" address the manner or way of things, the state of their condition, and the extent of subjects. "How Questions" are important in determining the processes of the past, present and future. "How should we do this?" looks at what steps are needed to go forward. "How Questions" often follow other questions. Once you determine your objective, your next question likely will be "How do I achieve this objective?" Consider these "How Questions" and how they apply to your life:

- How should I begin?
- How do I want to be remembered?
- How will this affect me?

- How will this affect others?
- How did this come to be?
- How are you?
- How do I get out of this?
- How much does it cost?
- How much do you care?
- How much do you have?
- How do you do that?
- How does that work?
- How will I know?
- How much did you pay?
- How do you feel?

**Would Questions**

"Would Questions" examine the potential of the future. "Would you like to go to the park?" "Would Questions" ask the recipient whether they want something and they look at how others might react to different situations. Examine these "Would Questions" and the different situations where they might apply:

- Would you like to try this?
- Would you do that?
- Would you believe this?
- Would it matter?
- Would they care?
- Would it make me a better person?
- Would it make me closer to my objectives?
- Would it improve the situation?
- Would it do any good?
- Would you rather?

Not all questions begin with "Who," "Why," "What," "Where," "When," "How," and "Would," but many do. Consider the objectives of your question and then examine how to best phrase it. What are you hoping to learn? What is your objective? Always ask yourself first why you are talking, and then choose the best form for your question.

**Affective Assessment**

Assessing how an individual feels about their circumstances is important in many different circumstances. How does a client feel about their working environment? How do they feel about your role with their company? Affective assessment calls for open-ended questions. Consider some of the following and answer them yourself. How would they apply in different situations?

- What are your thoughts?
- Why do you feel this way?
- What is most important to you? Why?

**Psychomotor Assessment**

Psychomotor assessment determines how tools are being incorporated and how applications are being conducted. Questions like these help to assess the processes of the working environment and where there's room for improvement. These questions apply in many job situations, but they also apply equally in life situations. Consider these questions and apply them to your life as a whole. What have you learned and how do you apply that knowledge?

- What has the product, service, or situation taught you?

- What areas need improvement?

- How can these areas be improved?

- How can functionality be further developed?

**Why Closed-Ended Questions Matter**

It can be easy to forget the importance of the closed-ended question. Quite often, we gain more information from an open-ended question than we do from a closed-ended question. "What are your thoughts on this matter?" leaves the ballpark completely open, whereas "Do you think we should fire John?" elicits a "yes" or "no" response. Closed-ended questions are questions in which the person can answer with one of several options. Closed-ended questions are important when decisions must be nailed down. When it comes down to deadlines, we often need that simple "yes" or "no" to determine whether we move forward or not. Sometimes the easy answer can be hard to get – and some individuals evade questions better than others. In these situations, using a closed-ended question is imperative.

- What is our decision today?

- Is this a yes or a no?

- What conclusion have we reached?

Knowing why you're asking a question is important in how you ask it. Examine what objective you're seeking, what type of response you're looking for, and how you'll use this information. In the next chapter, we'll look at how to use this information through asking more questions.

# Simple Rules for Communication

**Direct, Concise, and Simple**

Direct: "proceeding in a straight line or by the shortest course; straight; undeviating; not oblique."

Concise: "expressing or covering much in few words; brief in form but comprehensive in scope; succinct; terse."

Simple: "easy to understand, deal with, use, etc." (Dictionary.com)

Why is it important to be direct, concise, and simple when you pose questions and communicate? The reason is largely one of clarity. If you want to make a clear point or receive clear answers, it's imperative that you ask clear questions. Questions that contain multiple questions within them can be confusing. Questions that are vague will receive vague answers. "How are you?" barely elicits a response from most of us beyond "Fine. How are you?" "How was your vacation to Florida?" on the other hand can open the door to a conversation.

**Direct.** Why is "direct" important? I don't want to come off sounding like some kind of dictator! Don't worry. Being direct has nothing to do with being brash or harsh. Think of "direct sentence structure." Direct sentences involve a subject, an object, and a verb. "The boy hit the tree." is an example of a direct sentence. An indirect sentence, by contrast, would be, "The tree was hit by the boy." Both sentences work and are effective at portraying the situation. Direct sentences, however, are generally easier to understand. Don't garble up your words and make the other person need translation to understand your meaning. Speak directly.

Likewise, another obstacle that we often face in being direct with questions and communication is when we try to sound more intelligent than we are. You may, in fact, have the intelligence quotient of Albert Einstein, but unless you are able to communicate your ideas with others, you won't reach Einstein's success. Don't "dumb down" your thoughts for your audience - just be direct with them.

**Concise.** Why is being "brief in form but comprehensive in scope" important? Like being direct, being concise clarifies meaning. What achievement are you proudest of in your life? This sentence is brief, but the scope it covers it vast. I'm asking you to look at the entirety of your life experiences and pick one that stands out to you as something you are most proud of?

**Simple.** If you're being direct and concise, you should be simple. These three rules go hand in hand. Once you begin complicating one element, the rest will follow. Keep it simple. People in today's world, more than ever before, live on a limited sense of time. We eat on the go, multi-task, and communicate quickly. The simpler things are, the faster they are.

**Focus and Intent**

Focus and intent are important when asking questions because they indicate your objective. Why are you asking the question and what do you hope to attain from doing so? This is implied through focus and intent. Focus and intent are particularly important when a question may have multiple answers – or when multiple questions are present. Staying focused means keeping the eye on the ball and knowing how to ask one question at a time.

**Focus.** The ability to focus is important in all situations. This ability is threatened the most when many people are collaborating, when a project is multi-faceted and has multiple stages, and when dealing with long-term objectives. Focus essentially means locking in on one aspect of a larger whole. This is important, because every problem has multiple sub-problems. Delineating each step along the way can ensure that you can see "both the forest and the trees," so to speak. Focus is important when you're communicating because it can become easy to lose track and become distracted by the multitudes of minor sidesteps that occur along the way.

**Intent.** Intent goes back to your objective. Why are you communicating with this person, and what do you want from them? Your intent should be clear in your question. "Do you want to try A or B?" The intent with this question is for the other person to choose. "How do you feel about that?" The intent is for the person to share.

## W.A.I.T. = Why Am I Talking?

The acronym W.A.I.T. applies to almost every situation, although it commonly arises in parenting advice and guidelines. W.A.I.T. = Why Am I Talking? This question is important because it ties directly to your objective. The answer to this question often IS your objective. Why am I talking? Why am I asking? Why - is the ultimate "objective" question. We do things because we want certain results. The results are our objective. W.A.I.T applies in all situations because we should always know our objective. Before we begin to speak, whether to make a statement or pose a question, we need first to *listen.* We need to observe the other person and take in what they are relating to us. ***By listening, we allow different things to happen:***

1. We gain a greater understanding of the circumstances and situation.

2. We appear to CARE. We are not bulldozing our way through life and crushing others with our opinions. A wise man once said: "Listen to many, speak to a few." – William Shakespeare

W.A.I.T also applies in situations where you lose your cool. This is likely why it applies to the parent-child relationship so often. W.A.I.T = Why Am I Talking? Are you talking because you're angry? Then stop and examine your intentions. When we're angry, we often lash out to hurt others. Why? Because we want to change their behavior; because we want them to feel badly; because we feel the need for revenge; because we want to knock them down a peg; *because because because.*

Lashing out at someone from a place of

anger rarely accomplishes any real objective. If you want to change the behavior of someone - be them your child, spouse, coworker or boss, remember W.A.I.T. *Why am I talking? What is my objective?* If your objective is to change the behavior of someone else, examine ways to do that. Don't just look at the immediate gratification of being right or belittling. These attempts won't successfully change behavior like thoughtful reasoning will. "What have you learned from this situation?" may be an appropriate question here. At the very least, it will be more effective than "You idiot! How could you possibly do something so stupid!?"

The importance of listening should go without saying, but quite often in life it does not. If you ask a question, listen to the answer. ***Really listen.*** Don't plan your next question, prepare your argument, or anticipate the answer. **<u>Just listen.</u>** Actually take in what the other person is sharing with you. Listening means more than simply attuning your ears to comprehend words. Listen to the person's body language; listen to the tone of their voice. Listen to the emotions that you can sense coming from this person. Take in all of these elements and take the time to examine them.

Pausing is not a bad thing. Don't be so afraid of silence that you must fill it with mindless chatter. Allow the ideas of the person you're communicating with resonate in your mind and then respond. If you don't understand their response, ask them to clarify. Most of us would rather someone ask us what we mean than for them to stare blankly at us and then walk away without having taken in a single word.

**Know What to Do with the Answer**

This goes along with listening. If you ask a question, you should know how to deal with the answer. You should think this out before the question is posed. If you have no clue as to what to do with the answer, why are you asking the question? Consider different approaches to the answer. What is the next step? Follow-up questions should help you to determine your process to proceed.

In the next two chapters, we'll look at how the act of questioning can be applied in different situations, from work, to home, to social interactions. These "Simple Rules of Communication" will apply in every circumstance. Always remember to be direct, concise, and simple, ask your questions with focus and intent, W.A.I.T., and know what to do with the answer.

# **Communication in the Workplace**

Communication skills are vital in the workplace, regardless of whether you are an independent contractor, a member of a sales force, a CFO, a CEO, a union organizer, or a courier. Even authors, painters, and other predominantly solitary professions require some amount of communication – be it to one's literary agent or accountant.

In the workplace, the objectives behind our communication are often simpler: we're on a collective mission to accomplish an established objective. However, communicating that objective and staying on the same page are important. In this chapter, we'll look at the different questions of the workplace and the reasons some questions work better than others. These questions apply whether you're a schoolteacher, an auto mechanic, or an investment banker. Consider the circumstances, always know your objective, and examine how you can better face the workplace through asking questions!

**The Questions of the Job Interview**

There is no way around it. All of us who are in the workplace today must face the job interview at some point. Even if you're fortunate enough to be self-employed, you've sat on one side of the table or the other at least once. The job interview, like the first date, is all about questions. It's one of several situations that revolve solely around the process of asking and answering, and it's often one of the most important. There's a reason that there are more seminars, webinars, online courses, and other training in this one area than most others: In order to get a job, you have to know how to answer questions. I contend that in addition to that, in order to get a job, you have to know how to answer and ASK questions. In this section, we're going to look at both sides of the table-- that of the employer and of the potential employee. From both perspectives, you will see that knowing how to pose questions - and the right ones - is essential.

Whether you are an employer or someone seeking a job, the first thing that you should do is pose questions to yourself. This goes along with most situations, but in a job interview process, it is that much more important that you enter the situation knowing your answers. In a job interview, no one is going to take a 10-minute intermission while you sort through your thoughts and come up with an articulate answer. Many questions in the job interview situation are meant to take you off guard, however. Thus, knowing the answers to these questions before you enter the room puts you that much further ahead of your competition.

Knowing what you are looking for in an employee and knowing how to ask the right questions can mean the difference between hiring and firing five different replacements until the "right candidate" finally floats in the door - and hiring the "right candidate" in your first interview. According to Forbes Magazine, "[s]tudies show that a quarter of new hires wash out within one year and nearly half by 18 months." Not great odds. But what if you knew how to ask questions that could really give you the insight and foresight to see that a candidate is the "right" or the "wrong" person for the job?

First, let's take a look at some of the most common interview questions. As a potential employee, knowing the answers to these questions will get you far - but not, perhaps, completely in the door. Knowing what to expect in the average interview, though, can give you insight - and help you formulate your own questions for the employer. Because let's admit it: most of us go into job interviews powerless. It's important to remember that you're interviewing them as much as they are interviewing you. I'm sure I'm not alone in saying that I've been to a fair share of interviews in which I discovered halfway through that I didn't actually want this job at all. It wasn't the right "fit." So how do you determine that before you've spent six months working at a firm you detest? By asking the right questions at the interview!

Here are some of the most common questions posed in job interviews:

- What were your favorite aspects of your last job?

- Why did you leave your last job?

- What are your strengths?

- What are your weaknesses?

- Where did you study?

- What did you least like about your last job?

- Why are you interested in working for us?

- How did you hear about us?

- Can you explain why this gap exists on your resume?

- What are your goals?

There are many variations of these questions. What are your answers for each of them? If you were interviewed right now, could you answer each of these questions effectively?

Now let's consider some more questions that might be posed in an interview. These questions are more effective. Consider the following questions suggested by Forbes Magazine in an August, 2011 article titled "The Best Interview Questions You Never Ask" (8/3/2011):

- Tell me about our company.

- What are the first five things you would do if you got this job?

- What do you need in order to be successful in this job?

- Describe a time you took a risk and failed, and one where you took a risk and succeeded. What were the differences?

- What was one of your proudest moments at work?

- How does this position help you reach

your long-term goals?

How are these questions different? First, they're more specific, while still enveloping a wide scope. Remember the rules of "Direct, Concise, and Simple"? These questions and statements ask about long-term goals, personal habits, and the candidate's past experiences in a specific way while staying simple. The first questions - the most common questions - accomplish this goal as well, but many of the questions are very vague. Still others elicit little response. One of the best ways in dealing with generalized questions like the first examples is knowing how to specify by asking questions. Here's an example:

"What are your goals?" "Would you like to know about my goals specifically within this facet of the industry, or are you interested in hearing about my goals beyond that?" Now what does the interviewer think? "Oh, you have goals beyond this area. What are your larger goals?"

Before you step foot in the door, prepare yourself by asking yourself the common interview questions. Even more importantly, develop a list of questions of your own. If I could go back in time, I'd have done this for every interview I've failed at because I truly believe it's a deal-breaker. Write a list of 3-4 questions for the employer. Use these questions not only to inquire about the company's work style, but also to show that you've put effort into researching them. "What are your feelings about the recent merger, and how does that affect your mission statement here?"

Ask questions regarding specific areas of development as well as questions that look at the overall work ethic of the employees. When it comes down to that inevitable "Do you have any questions for us?" don't just sit there blankly, trying to review your performance and determine how well you've impressed the gatekeeper - ask them about what they believe your position contributes to the overall goals of the company! Ask them questions about what their goals are and how they want to progress in the future. Ask how you can contribute to that. Ask them, "What did you feel were the areas most lacking in the previous employee who filled this role?" "What do you think is the most important element of this job?"

Asking questions from a potential employee perspective during the job interview is as important as the potential employer asking questions. It shows that you're not desperate. It shows that you are actively evaluating whether you are willing and interested in working with a company or individual. It shows that you care enough to dig in and do some basic research and are looking at the long-term goals of the company. And that will get their attention.

**Before you go into a job interview, ask yourself the following:**

**If you are an employer:**

- What qualities are important to me for this position?

- What are the job duties of this position and who would best fulfill those?

- What is the role of this position within the greater whole of the company?

- What team members will be interacting with this individual the most? What are their requirements for the position?

- How much opportunity for growth is there in this position?

**If you are the potential employee:**

- What qualities are important to me for this position?

- How does the "team" work together?

- What will be the greatest areas of

difficulty in this work?

- What kind of growth opportunity is there in this position?

- What are the most important aspects of the job from my interviewer's point of view?

**Employer-Employee Relationships**

Once you've gotten the job, your work is obviously far from over - it's just begun. The process of communication is always continuing, and you need to ensure that you're on the same page as your employer or your employees. The best way to do this is - again - knowing how to ask the right questions and when. As a new employee, you're bound to be filled with questions at this point - from "Where is my desk?" to "What do you expect of me?"

In order to effectively assimilate yourself into the new workplace, you must ask questions. What we often forget, though, is to keep asking questions even after we're accustomed to the location of the break room or the way certain employees operate. Consider the following questions from an employer and an employee standpoint. Ask yourself these questions and ask your employer or employees for their feedback as well. Listen to the responses you get – either from yourself or from others – and ask follow-up questions. "Why?" can be posed after every one of the following:

**From an employee perspective:**

- How do you feel about my performance?
- What would you like to see me focus more on?
- In what ways does my work contribute to the overall goals of the company?
- How do you think I can make a greater contribution?

**From an employer perspective:**

- What issues are coming up? How do we deal with them in the best way?
- What can we do to make your work more productive?
- What area of the job excites you the most? What excites you the least?
- What have you learned from the

situation?

By asking questions, we can ensure that we're meeting our employer's and employees' expectations. Why spend a year waiting for yearly evaluations to know you're doing your job well or not? If you're proactive, you want to meet his or her expectations now and understand the ways in which you can improve and get ahead. Next, we'll examine ways to keep the lines of communication clear within employee-employee teams.

**Employee-Employee Relationships**

Not every job position is a member of a "team," but the majority are. Even if you're a small organization, you likely have different "teams" within your company – from marketing teams to product development teams to sales teams. We interact within specific teams for a corporation at times and we communicate with members of other teams.

No one enjoys "office politics." Office politics usually arises from a lack of communication in the workplace. This lack of communication, in turn, develops into hidden resentments, jealousies, petty arguments, and the emergence of "office cliques." When office politics starts turning into "office dramas," you've got a full-fledged problem on your hands. What may have started as a single minor resentment can eventually pull a whole company under. Don't believe me? Ask any number of companies that have collapsed in the past year whether office politics played a part in their downfall. Chances are those "minor internal squabbles" played as big or bigger a role than an economic downturn did.

According to a 2012 article from WebFinance, Inc. titled "Organizational Politics," "Workplace politics is the use of power within an organization for the pursuit of agendas and self-interest without regard to their effect on the organization's efforts to achieve its goals." Thus, the deviation from the company's objective – or "mission" – is the key problematic element in office politics. If the energy used to implement those "self-serving interests" were instead applied to the objectives of the company, great progress would be made. The ultimate question then becomes: "How do we prevent and or/stop office politics from occurring?"

The first step in preventing office politics from taking control is to establish and maintain both communication and acknowledgment within all facets of the organization. If each company member is aware of how their role contributes to the whole – and they are acknowledged for their contributions – petty jealousies are less likely to occur. When one team member is given "favorite status" from the boss – things can begin to go awry.

What if that "boss's favorite" happens to be you? How do you deal with the unspoken but tangible resentment of those around you when you feel picked from the crowd as an example of excellence? Without demeaning yourself or your own contributions, acknowledge others who assisted in your achievement. "Thank you, but I really couldn't have done it without ____ 's help" will go a long way in creating a hospitable environment with those around you.

Another important aspect of teamwork to remember is to ask how you can be of help to others. The favorite employee in any workplace is most often the one who finishes their work and asks, "Is there any way I can help you with that?" as opposed to the worker who quickly clocks out and is halfway home before you can even ask for their assistance. If your fellow employees are working on a project that isn't your specialty, ask how you might be of assistance! Even if you can't help, you'll be remembered as the person who asked. One of the biggest questions to ask yourself in order to thwart the deadly grip of office politics is "How will this help achieve the company's objectives?" If the answer is "It won't," then consider what your driving force really is.

### The Questions of the Sales Pitch

In any arena you enter, you should know why you're communicating and what you hope to accomplish. It is important to ask yourself, before you ever ask *them,* "Why am I asking?" "Who am I asking?" "What do I want?" This is especially true in sales. Why? Because people who are regularly solicited *to buy* are well versed in the use of "sales tricks" and many of them will toss you out the door before you get two questions out.

We all *sell something* at some point. In the job interview situation, we're selling ourselves. "Is this company a great fit for me?" "What do I have that they want?" Selling, of course, extends beyond the interview to products, advertising, representation, services—even *ideas* are bought and sold regularly. If your job revolves primarily around the act of *selling,* you're well aware that there are many elements of your job that require you to communicate well.

There are four principle questions that

will help you predetermine whether a sale will take place. Before you even make the effort to step through the door, you must ensure you're stepping through the right one! A perfectly executed sales pitch demonstrated for the wrong individual will get you no further than a bad sales pitch to the right individual. Prepare yourself, do the essential research, and answer each of the following questions before you begin:

### Does the buyer have a problem that the product addresses?

There's an old metaphor about how a good salesman can sell ice to an Eskimo. While this may be valid in extreme cases, generally speaking, you're not going to sell an Eskimo any ice – or any Rogaine to a Yeti, for that matter. Is your product something that the buyer will use? If not, find another buyer! Direct your sales efforts toward those who have a need for your products or services. If the buyer does not perceive there being any problem with their current situation, why should they throw money at you? Your job is to show them *HOW* your product solves their problem. How can you do this best? By asking questions! Your potential buyer may not see a problem, but your "pointing out" the problem won't be as effective as asking them questions that lead them to the realization for themselves. "You say your computer boot-up time takes you approximately 20 seconds, is that right? How much time do you think you could save each day if I told you we could get your startup time down to 5 seconds? What could you do with the extra time spent staring at the red light?"

## Is there dissatisfaction with the current offerings or their development?

If the problem is "there's dirt in my carpet," and the solution is "use a vacuum cleaner," then the next question invariably becomes "which one?" If the vacuum cleaner that you're currently using satisfies your needs completely, you have no reason to buy another – and no dirt on the floor. Ask yourself before you walk through the door, "What does my product or service offer that the competition does not?" "In what areas is the competition lacking?" "How great is this buyer's satisfaction with the competition?" "Are there ways that I can question the buyer in order to determine where their dissatisfaction lies?"

**Is the buyer personally invested in the problem?**

The reason that soap operas exist is to sell soap to housewives. The advertising that oozes from the TV between the hours of 9 a.m. and 3 p.m. is notoriously sudsy. Why? Surely, we know that in today's world there are plenty of men who are stay-at-home caregivers while their wives step out into the workplace. Regardless of this, though, you'll rarely find a slew of commercials for stereotypically "macho" items at this time of day. Does this mean that your typical American household doesn't have needs for both laundry detergent AND power tools? Of course not. They're simply directing their sale at the person most concerned with the problem that their product addresses.

Is the buyer capable of making decisions on this matter? Are they at a level of clearance to "buy"? If not, speak to the person who is. You can spend three hours selling a marketing campaign to a receptionist before they finally say, "But I don't make decisions on that matter. My boss does." Ask this question to yourself before you go in, and ask it of the individual you're speaking to. "Are you the person I should be discussing this with? Are there others who need to be involved in the decision-making process? Is it possible to speak with them as well?"

**Does the buyer trust you (your company and your product) are the best solution?**

Trust goes a long way in the world of business. Developing trust between buyer and seller is an ultimate goal—and this applies from the top tier of decision-makers to the grocery store shopper on Wednesday afternoon. Your choice to repeatedly purchase the same deodorant brand is based on "buyer trust." Why do you choose to buy X Brand? *Because you've used it before and it worked well.* You therefore trust it will work well again.

Trust between the buyer and the seller is

generated in many ways. One way, in the example above, is proven product satisfaction. If the product keeps fulfilling its required role, I'm not that likely to start "shopping around" for different deodorant brands. It works – why fix it? Another way that buyer trust is established is through advertising. Specifically, celebrity advertising, which uses a "spokesperson" to vouch for a product, can develop buyer trust because if they trust that celebrity, they're perhaps give the product a shot. "Betty White said this deodorant works. I trust Betty White. I'll try this deodorant."

If you're selling a buyer on a product or service, you're Betty White. If you walk into the door looking like the Big Bad Wolf, I'm going to be very wary of anything that comes out of your mouth. If you're Betty White, I'm going to give you a chance. I might even open up to you, if you ask the right questions.

What questions do you ask a buyer in order to develop trust? Try some of the following. Remember, though: Don't attempt to use a prescribed set of questions and answers with every buyer in every situation. If you pay enough attention to the rule of **listening**, you'll find that your conversation will flow freely to further questions. If you're using a "script" and pay no attention to the buyer's answers, you're not only getting nowhere in terms of addressing their concerns, but you're also coming off like a shyster and are shooting yourself in the foot. Never forget to listen and respond!

- How did you get interested/started in this industry?

- How does X relate to the company's mission/objectives?

- What would make your job easier?

- What are some of the most difficult aspects of your job?

- What do you value most with X product?

- What dissatisfactions do you have with X product?

- How do you feel this decision will

affect your team?

- What is the most important thing we should discuss today?

- What are your thoughts on that?

If your answers to the four principle questions above give you pause, examine them. Know who your buyer is and why they should buy from you. And be sure to listen!

# **Choosing the Right Mode of Communication is Key!**

In today's world, we have an ever-expanding selection of modes of communication at our disposal. Email, snail mail, telephone, faxes, cell phones, internet chat, and video chat are the most common. In the workplace, we often make use of any or all of these modes of communication in order to do our jobs—but knowing which one to use when is an important step that's often overlooked.

We all have "favorite" modes of communication. Some of us write well and enjoy the ability to develop our thoughts through emails; others prefer face-to-face connection; still others can talk on the phone for hours at a time. Knowing the best mode of communication for each individual you regularly deal with can make a huge difference in the workplace. In this chapter, we're going to look at the different qualities of each of the main modes of communication and why some are better than others at certain times.

**Snail Mail**

Let's start with taking a look at the oldest

among the modes of communication aside from face-to-face discussion. People have written letters for centuries and for the first time in history, snail mail is vastly outnumbered by many faster, easier methods used to stay in touch. That doesn't mean that snail mail is extinct yet, though! In fact, old-fashioned letters are still a valuable tool and should be regarded as such. They are a necessity in many aspects of the job, including quite often contracts that must be signed, legal paperwork that must be submitted, and advertising.

We often forget that the effort put into mailing resumes, contracts, letters of inquiry, etc. shows the person we're communicating with that we are willing to make that effort. A resume in the mail may stand that much higher in the stack compared with those submitted via email – because, let's face it, it's easy to overlook emails, especially when they often are sent straight to your spam folder. In the acting industry, casting directors and agents have complained in the past several years that their headshot/resume stacks are now empty. It's great, they assert, that actors have become internet-savvy in terms of how they promote themselves, but casting directors are that much more likely to overlook an actor who submits via email because it's just easy to delete them. The same applies to resumes submitted to a variety of industries – when submitting resumes, a hard copy is more impressive. Sure, some companies only accept emailed submissions (and that's fine) – but if you have the option, mail it with a stamp.

The same applies for letters of gravity, thank-you notes, and birthday cards. Are you one tenth as pleased when you receive "Happy Birthday!" greetings on Facebook as you are when you receive a card in the mail? Which shows more effort? If someone has sent you a gift, send them a card to say thanks – after all, they took the effort to get you something; the least you can do is lick a stamp in return.

Snail mail does have its drawbacks, of course. Otherwise, it wouldn't be overshadowed by the telephone and email. You cannot receive fast responses from snail mail – so if you're making a proposal that must be agreed on today – you should obviously choose a faster mode of communication. If a contract must be signed, there are a number of different options including scanners, faxes, and email. Snail mail is the communication mode of choice when it comes to letters of recommendation, resumes, cover letters, thank-you notes, holiday cards, and important contracts. Keep this in mind in your work.

**Email**

Email is one of the fastest and most convenient methods of communication – so it's not hard to discern why it's so popular. If you need a quick answer to a question, email can be great. It also has drawbacks, though. Email is tricky and if you're not careful, you can end up in a spam folder and your message will never be read. If you're emailing someone for the first time, ensure that they know to expect your email by placing a telephone call as well. This is advantageous when applying for jobs where an emailed resume is preferred. You can quickly call the receptionist or HR person at the company and let them know you've emailed a resume and that you wanted to make sure you had the correct address.

Email can be impersonal. It's easy to send out blanket messages to hundreds of people at once – in fact, those emails are most often quickly sent to spam folders. Bulk emails are little better than the junk mail that piles up on your kitchen table. Sure, once in a blue moon will you sort through it and find the grocery store coupons, but once you do, they're likely already expired. If you have an important contract to discuss or propose, email should be one of the last modes of communication you choose. If you're already agreed and simply tweaking details, email can be fine – but in terms of posing "big" questions, face-time is always a better choice.

That said, though, many of us spend the majority of our workday sending and receiving emails. Knowing how to communicate in an effective way is important when you're talking in the virtual world – because words can be misconstrued, meanings can be misinterpreted, and petty conflicts can arise easily. Emails in the workplace should be considered as seriously as any other mode of communication. Unless you'd draw a smiley-face on an inter-office memo, don't do it in your emails. Although emails are not as formal as letters or contracts, they should still be professional. Use proper grammar, punctuation, and save the emoticons for your messages to friends.

In today's world, a growing number of us work from home. Because of this, email is as important as sitting down with your boss or team members in the conference room. Email is a way to convey ideas quickly and to quickly get feedback. Knowing how to ask questions in email is likewise important. The same rules apply here as before:

A.   Direct, concise, and simple.

B. Focus and intent.

C. W.A.I.T. = Why Am I Talking?

D. Know what to do with the answer.

If you're writing an email to a team member to discuss options for how to deal with any number of obstacles, email is fine. Pose your questions directly, clearly, and simply. Make sure the other person understands the question! Make your focus and intent clear. What do you intend to do with the information? How will it further each of your objectives? Listening. We cannot easily show we are listening via email, but there are ways to get that message across. When you receive your message, ensure that you show you understand their response. Repeat it back to them and address the different aspects of it. Show that you've put time and thought into their information by acknowledging it and possibly asking more specific questions relating to their response.

Know what to do with the answer. Again, don't ask a question if you have no idea what to do with the answer. Be able to use the information to further your objectives. Consider asking questions like: "What are your thoughts on that?" "How do you think we should go forward, given this information?" "What would you like to see more of?" Then, acknowledge their responses and deepen the discussion. Email is an invaluable tool in today's workplace. Knowing how to properly address emails for the given circumstances is essential. If you struggle with emails, invest in a business etiquette guide and study it. Learning to communicate effectively using the internet will vastly improve your success in the workplace.

**Telephone**

Land-line phones. Cell phones. Smart phones. Conference calls. The technology of telephones is another realm that has evolved steadily over the past thirty years. Long gone are the days of a single land-line in a home; most people today communicate via cell phone. Like with email, this expanding technology has complicated things to a degree. When is an appropriate time to call? What number do you call? How many people will be involved in the call? These are all questions you should answer when you pick up the telephone—be it your smart phone, your office line, or your home phone.

What is the purpose of your communication? Are you discussing the development of a marketing campaign, scheduling an interview, establishing business connections, or proposing a contract? Telephones supersede emails because they're more personal. A client is more likely to discuss a pending sale via the telephone than via email. It is easier to determine a person's reservations, subtext, and excitement over the phone. For these reasons and more, phone conversations are an important aspect of the workplace.

If you're posing questions to a fellow teammate, your employer, or a client, you can learn much more from them by telephone. When responding to an email, we have time to sort out our thoughts, place emphasis as needed, and evaluate what we're conveying. Telephone conversations are much more direct and spontaneous. You can tell if a person stammers when answering a question on the phone, and you can adjust your inquiries accordingly. "How willing is my client to invest in this venture?" You can much more effectively test the waters by calling and analyzing their voice than you can by letter or email.

Of course, nothing beats face-to-face contact, but a telephone call is far more personal than an email or a standard letter. Because telephone conversations are more intimate, however, you should also be aware of telephone etiquette. If you're conducting business, choose a business number to reach your client, coworker, or boss. Don't call their personal cell phone at 9 p.m. to discuss a project—unless, of course, they've suggested it. We all value our private time away from the office and it can be difficult remember that everyone is not "on call" 24-hours a day.

If you're working on a team with an approaching deadline and you must call to discuss matters outside of office hours, ensure that this is anticipated by the team. Also, evaluate your team members, employers, and clients to determine how they best communicate. Is this person a "phone talker" or do they "clam up" on the phone? Calling a client to propose a sale when the client is uncomfortable on the phone can be deadly. You're better off calling to schedule an in-person meeting. If you need to bounce ideas off a team member and they are comfortable chatting on the phone, by all means, call them.

What about conference calls? Conference calls are another excellent method of communicating with teams, and they likewise have rules of etiquette. Ensure that you are clear, direct, and simple when communicating via conference call. It can be easy for signals to be crossed and for interruptions to occur. When you pose questions via conference call, make sure that the recipient of the question is indicated.

"Mr. Smith, what are your thoughts on that?" "Ms. Roberts, what is the position of the sales team at this point?" Know what individuals are involved in the call, and know who is speaking at all times.

**Scanners and Faxes**

Fax machines are still used today, but they've become largely overshadowed by scanners in the past decade. Both are important in terms of getting contracts signed quickly, submitting resumes and cover letters, and communicating objectives. If you're working with charts, diagrams, objective outlines, or other visual elements, scanners and faxes are important in conveying ideas.

**Internet Chat and Text Messaging**

Chatting online is quicker than email and can be a great tool for discussing ideas with team members. It is the least formal of technological communication methods, and should be reserved for situations that are appropriate. Unless you regularly discuss projects with your clients via web chat, use another method when bringing up major issues. The same applies for text messaging. Texting someone can be a great way to communicate when you're setting up meeting times, arranging travel plans, or posing quick questions. Texting and web chat are NOT appropriate for establishing major initiatives. Don't be Britney Spears and hire or fire someone via text message. It's tacky. If it's important, set up a time to discuss it in person.

**Video Chat**

Video chat (Skype.com, ooVoo.com, Google Chat, etc.) is an excellent method of communication in today's workplace. Video chat combines the elements of the telephone and email with face-to-virtual-face contact. It is the best method for communicating when you need that intimate connection but cannot be in the same place at the same time. The only main drawback to video chat is that it's relatively new and not all people are set up for it. Technical problems like bad internet connections can get in the way. But, if your clients and your team are comfortable with video chat, make use of it.

**Social Media**

If you don't believe that social media is

around to stay, I'd have to ask you to show me any product from a grocery store that doesn't have a Facebook page. Even potatoes have a Facebook page today. Seriously: https://www.facebook.com/pages/Potatoes. Facebook and its predecessors, Friendster, MySpace, and others, have revolutionized the way that we interact and communicate on a massive scale. Social media has not only changed our interactions with each other, it's also changed the face of advertising. Knowing how to use social media to your benefit can mean the difference between career options and friendships; conversely, NOT knowing how to effectively communicate through social media can mean uncomfortable face-offs, ended friendships, and needless squabbles. Social media can be your ally or your enemy.

The impact of social media in the workplace can be seen by the many lawsuits and policy changes every day in the news. According to a January, 2013 article from technorati.com titled "Social Media: Workplace Cool or Ultimate Firing Tool?" author David Goehst asserts, "Since certain verbiage usage has 5th Amendment protection, canning someone for discussing how John spilled spaghetti inside company break rooms – provided it doesn't impede work performance – isn't punishable. Showing pictures of secured areas, however, which only certain employees (and eyes) have clearance to view still remains a huge no-no."

Social media in the workplace is a tricky thing. Currently, two states (California and Illinois) prevent employers from requesting a potential or current employee's passwords to sites like Facebook and other networking sites. But how do you balance the line between "friendship" and "professionalism" when it comes to social media? Will your boss be peeved if you don't answer his "friend request"? What about your clients? And what information do you share with these individuals if you *do* accept that friend request?

Some friends I know have set up two different accounts – one for "friends" and one for "work." This can be effective if, like them, you're a college professor. Utilizing social media in order to communicate study assignments, upcoming tests, or even to continue class discussions can be great, but you don't also necessarily want to share your party pictures from last weekend with your students. You can also set up a "public figure" page, like other friends I know who are actors, directors, writers, or artists. These pages can be "liked" but remain separate from your personal social media page. These pages are effective for anyone in the public arena because they allow you to maintain your personal privacy while updating the latest information regarding film releases, performances, or book publications.

If you don't want to establish a separate social media page for work, you can also adjust your privacy settings on Facebook and other sites in order to limit who sees what you post. Again, this can be tricky—especially as settings frequently evolve and change within the system. What appeared to be "private" may somehow become public – so it's best to ensure that you don't post *anything* that could potentially make you to lose your job. That means: **Don't post tirades about your boss or coworkers on Facebook.** If you need to vent, share a private conversation with friends. We often take for granted the interconnectedness of the world around us – especially in the world of social media. Even if you've ensured your boss is not your friend on a social media site, that doesn't mean his cousin-in-law can't see some passing remark you publically make about him.

Social media, in short, can help you or hurt you in the workplace. It is *not* a great tool for workplace communication – it is not as appropriate as email, video conferencing, telephone, or face-to-face contact. It can, however, be a great tool for the independent entrepreneur, the artist, the teacher, and the advertiser. Social media is an excellent promotional tool, and I suggest that those interested advancing their skills commit to further research on the subject. George Takei's book, *Oh Myyy! (There Goes the Internet)* is an excellent resource for understanding the nuances of social media and how to use it to your advantage. Moreover, Takei proves that we don't have to be teenagers in order to know how to navigate our way through the virtual universe – many of our grandparents are on Facebook, after all.

**Questions to Ask Yourself Before Communicating**

Whenever you prepare to communicate with someone in the workplace, ask yourself the following questions in order to determine what the best method for communication would be. Most often, face-to-face discussions prevail over all others in matters of seriousness. When you cannot speak face-to-face, ask yourself:

- Why am I posing this question or having this discussion?

- What is the objective?

- Do I need a "yes or no" response, or am I seeking extensive analysis?

- What is my time frame and when is the deadline?

- How is this person involved in the decision-making process?

- How does this individual communicate best? Are they a phone person, an email person, or a face-to-face person?

- What modes of communication are at my disposal? What modes of communication are at the other individual's disposal?

- Do I need to share an image, chart, diagram or other visual aid as part of my communication? What is the best method for sharing this information?

- Is this a casual discussion or a more formal discussion?

- How many individuals need to be part of this discussion?

When you've effectively answered these questions, you should have little question regarding the best method for communication. Prepare your correspondence accordingly, and be sure you listen and acknowledge their response!

Adjusting how you communicate with others is a continual process. Some days, you may elicit nothing from someone over the phone, but when you step into their office, it's a different matter. Listening is the key to making adjustments. How open is this individual using this method of communication? What should I do in order to ensure they actually understand me? Is there a better way to discuss this subject? If so, make an adjustment! Ask if you can schedule a meeting with him/her at a convenient time, or arrange to discuss matters on video chat when they are available. If you're perceptive, you'll be able to sense the best approach.

In the following chapter, we'll take questions and communication from the office to the home. Much of the same information applies, although our objectives may differ substantially when we're dealing with our spouse as opposed to our coworkers. The key to communication – *listening* – applies whether we're at the dining table, the parent-teacher conference, or the office.

# **Communication with Friends and Family**.

For many of us, communication with our friends and family comes naturally – but not for everyone. Knowing how to use questions can change your friendships, acquaintanceships, and intimate relationships considerably. Why? Because questions are a unique way to build bonds, understand individuals, relate to them, and connect.

If you've ever had a friend who consistently chatters about themselves without ever asking you how your day was – you know how tiring these individuals can be. A lack of questions and concern for others and their well-being is ultimately off-putting. If you're still friends with that self-centered chatterbox, chances are you don't spend that much time with them. People who inflict their lives on others without taking in those around them will eventually find themselves with no one to talk to.

Within the context of social communication, there are a number of different common "relationships" that factor into how you connect. There are "parent-child relationships," "spousal relationships," "friend relationships," "sibling relationships," and even "parent-teacher relationships." Within each of these specific relationships, your objectives will vary depending on circumstances. Communicating well, though, can mean the difference between having a child that's a problem student and having a connected objective of improvement between the parents, the child, and the teacher.

When we communicate well, we demonstrate our objectives clearly and we express our openness to others' opinions, objectives, and feelings. The "Simple Rules of Communication" apply here as much as in the workplace. Remember, just because we love someone does not mean we cannot have an objective when interacting with this person. Our objectives may be different, but they are still objectives. Always ask yourself "What do I want?" and "Why am I talking?" in every situation you encounter, and your objectives will always be clear to you.


**Family, Friends, Acquaintances, and Dates – Who are they and why do Questions Matter within these Relationships**

Who are your family, friends, acquaintances and dates? They're the people you interact with every day! Although we may have friends in the workplace, our processes of communication are generally different with those friends than the ones we've known for decades. We're more candid with our friends and loved ones. We often believe we don't have any objectives with these individuals – because we assume that to have a "hidden agenda" is a manipulative way to live. Objectives within relationships of love and friendship still exist – they are just different. You're not attempting "to sell" something to your spouse or your friends (or not usually); you're more likely attempting to connect with them. You may want to share your experiences and share in theirs. Sharing and listening are key components in our close relationships, and in this chapter, we'll look at how using questions can deepen those connections.

## The Family Unit – Communicating with Your Spouse and Children

Communication begins at home. The ways that we communicate with our spouse and children will influence these individuals for their lifetimes. Establishing clear communication in the home is essential for giving our children the basis of their own communication with friends, teachers, dates, and spouses down the line. Questions are at the heart of that communication.

When we're dating, questions come naturally. We are assessing the potential of an individual for a long-term commitment. Once we've gotten past this "initial dating phase," questions are just as important, but we often fail to realize it. If you scarcely scan the surface of relationship-improvement books, you'll find that the majority of relationship issues arise from a lack of communication. *Well, this is fine and good, but how do I improve my communication with my spouse?* Knowing how to ask open-ended questions and to truly listen to the person you love will take you far in terms of improving your connection. When is the last time you asked your husband or wife "What is important to you?" or "What dreams do you still hope to fulfill?"

We don't ask these questions of our loved ones often because we believe we know the answers. In reality, we all change, and what we may have longed for ten years ago may not be what we long for today. Our objectives change just as we do, and when one spouse's objectives suddenly take a left turn, it's important to know and to assess the situation.

Consider the following questions for your significant other and think of different ways these questions might be asked. Most importantly, though, listen to your spouse's response. Take in what they're saying and how it applies to your own hopes, dreams, and desires. Where are the areas of compromise?

- If you could live anywhere, where would you like to live? Why?

- What dreams do you still want to fulfill? What dreams and goals have you achieved?

- How should we begin to achieve these goals?

- What qualities do you want our children to embody? Why?

- What concerns you the most in our relationship?

- What is the most important aspect of our relationship to you?

- Where do you hope to be in X years? How do you envision this life?

When we raise children, they absorb our methods of communication. By asking questions, we show our children that we care about how they feel, think, and act. We also show them that asking questions is not only OK – it is important. Children and teenagers can test our patience with eye-rolling and ignoring us – and this is especially true when we "sermonize" or assert rules without also establishing the reasons for those rules.

The next time you're about to launch into a sermon about anything to your children, ask yourself "Why Am I Talking?" What do you hope to achieve? How can you best achieve this objective? Consider the following questions to pose to your children and examine how they differ from "sermonizing" or lecturing. How can these questions be used to change behavior, establish clarity of communication and objectives, and instill empathy in our children?

- What do you want to be when you grow up? Why? What about ___ are you passionate about?

- How do you feel about school? What subjects do you enjoy? Why do you enjoy them?

- How have you learned from X situation? What will you do next time? Why?

- How did that make you feel? Why?

- What do you want to achieve in the next X period of time? Why?

- What can I (or we) do to help you

achieve that?

- Who are your best friends? Why do you feel that way about them?

- What has made today special? What has made this time different?

By asking our children about their thoughts, desires, and feelings, we connect with them and we learn from them. Just because *you* understand the importance of schoolwork and establishing good friendships for your children doesn't mean that they do. Ask them what is important to them, and instill in them the ability to ask questions of others and of themselves.

Giving our children the ability to question will ultimately give them the attributes of empathy and compassion. Ask your children how they feel and how the actions of others have affected them. This way, they will ask themselves the same questions down the line. Ask them how their actions have affected others and how those people might feel. By asking questions, we learn not only schoolbook answers, but we gain insight into the minds of those around us. That insight is the foundation for compassion.

## Siblings, Parents, and Extended Family – Creating a Supportive Foundation with Questions

If communication begins in the home, you might be wondering "Well how do I make up for my own parents' lack of communication?" If you're lucky, you grew up with compassionate parents who cared about your thoughts, desires, and actions. They asked you what you thought about the world, about your friends, and about life. If your family was less communicative, you might feel trapped in that void. We can all establish bad communication habits, and many of them linger within the family. You might harbor resentment ten years after your brother ratted you out for sneaking out of the house as a teenager. You might feel extended teenage angst over your parents' lack of understanding for your goals and actions.

Can you amend a faulty line of communication within the family? Yes. Questions will help you do that. Just like with our spouses and children, our parents and siblings' objectives change over time. Have you considered asking your mother what her desires are after her children have all left home? Have you thought of what it might mean to your father if you asked him about his choices in life, his accomplishments, and his desires? What about your siblings? How have their lives changed in the course of growing up, marrying, having children, and establishing careers? What is important to them today, as opposed to yesterday?

Asking questions can open up lines of communication with your family beyond your expectations. As we grow older, our relationships with our parents and siblings change. Understanding what their desires are helps us to be supportive of them, and allows them to support us in turn. What does "family" mean to you, and how do you create that vision within your own family? Ask questions!

**Friends and Acquaintances – What's to Ask?**

Perhaps the better question here is "What's not to ask?" What is the level of communication you have with your friends? Do you discuss your love lives, sex lives, children, work, and hobbies? Are you "acquaintances" with someone that you share common interests, but you're not particularly close to on an intimate level? Asking our friends about their feelings and thoughts is as important as asking our family members and ourselves.

Questions tell others that we care how

they are doing, what they're thinking, and what they want. Remember the chatterbox friend I mentioned earlier? No one wants to be that person, but sometimes we become so caught up in our own lives and experiences that we forget to ask others what is going on with them. Take a moment when you're lost in conversation to consider how the other person feels. In fact, don't just consider it, but ask them!

Why do you ask questions from your friends? Consider your objectives. Do you want to understand this person on a deeper level? Do you want them to trust you? Do you want to illustrate that you care about them? Questions do all these things. Ask the "important questions" and listen to the response you get. "What do you care the most about?" "Why?" "What do you want the most from life?" "What would you like to have accomplished when you die?" I'm not suggesting that every conversation you have with friends and acquaintances will entail these questions – there's no reason to turn into a human Mad-Libs with an endless barrage of philosophical questions! However, if you ask your friends their thoughts and feelings about their lives, their work, their spouses, and their children, you're likely to engage them to share with you. More than anything, we want to know that our friends care about us, respect us, and care about our thoughts and feelings. Friendship is about sharing, and questions are an important aspect of that.

> "When we honestly ask ourselves which person in our lives means the most to us, we often find that it is those who, instead of giving advice, solutions, or cures, have chosen rather to share our pain and touch our wounds with a warm and tender hand."
>
> – Henri Nouwen

## Questions to Consider for Friends, Family, Acquaintances, and Dates

How do you begin to change your communication skills with your friends, acquaintances, and dates? By asking questions! Take the time to ask the opinions and thoughts of those you spend time with. Again, listening is the key. When you pose questions to friends, dates, or acquaintances, take time with their responses. Take in what they're really saying, and then respond with follow-up questions or comments.

Consider some of the following questions to pose to those you interact with on a social level. These questions have a multitude of different objectives, but generally speaking, they are questions used to open a person up. You're not looking at closed-ended questions in most situations with friends, unless the question is "Do you want Chinese or Mexican food for dinner?" Chances are, the people you pose these questions to will stop to think about their answers. That's a good thing! Sometimes, the questions posed by others lead us to questions we would like to know ourselves. Open-ended questions are a great tool in this regard.

- What has been the happiest day of your life? Why?

- What are your dreams? What goals do you still want to meet before you die?

- What are your feelings about X?

- What do you feel is the right decision for you? Why do you feel that way?

- What did you learn from X?

- What is your biggest passion in life? Why?

- What are the things that make you happy?

In our friendships and family relationships, there inevitably comes a time when you're asked for advice on a serious matter.

Perhaps your best friend is considering a divorce, or your brother asks you for advice about what college he should attend. Life changes are massive undertakings, and being cornered for advice can be a scary situation. What if you suggest the wrong solution?

In order to deal with major questions regarding life-changing events, consider asking "What do you feel is the right decision for you?" This question takes the pressure off yourself in order to listen as the other individual lists the pros and cons of their situation. Ultimately, they will be the one to decide, so why should you make a judgment before knowing any of the extenuating circumstances? Ask about the different aspects of their situation. Ask how they feel. Chances are, they've already answered their own question and are looking for feedback. Once you know where their mind is, you can more objectively look at their situation. Quite often, when we turn to our friends for their advice, we need someone to listen to us. So be that friend and listen!

# Communicating in a Modern World: Connecting with Friends, Family, and Love Interests via the Internet

There's no question that the way we communicate today is vastly different than communication styles and methods of one hundred years ago. The telephone and the internet have altered our world forever, and knowing how to communicate using these formats is as important in the realms of friendship, family, and dating, as it is in the workplace. In this chapter, we'll look at the nuances of communication in a virtual world.

**To Friend or Not to Friend? Online Communication with Friends and How to Navigate Your Way through Social Media**

*Facebook. Friendster. MySpace. Pinterest. Google Plus. Reddit. Skype. Groupon. Travelocity. Online Dating Sites.*

Social media has changed the way we interact with friends, family, coworkers, employers, students, and almost everyone around us. Regardless of whether you log onto a social media site once a day or once a week, you're still interacting on a virtual plane more than you were twenty years ago. How we interact within the constraints of social media affects us in our everyday lives, whether we'd like to admit it or not. From eliminating job prospects to ending long-term friendships, social media can have vast repercussions if used ineffectively.

You know that guy who you just "unfriended" because you got sick of his political posts? What if that former "friend" is your cousin that you sit next to every Thanksgiving dinner? Things might get uncomfortable. Likewise, imagine that you went on a rant about your coworker, only to discover that the supposedly "private" post was public? How do you deal with the aftermath?

The first approach is to not make those mistakes, obviously. Consider the repercussions of your online actions before you commit to them. Of course, this can be difficult when the invention of the "delete" button is so easy and fast to access. When you log on to a social media site, imagine that you're walking into a bar, party, or other social setting. Would you just walk up to someone and slap them? Most of us would not – but of course that depends on the circumstances. Consider your online interactions as "real" as your real interactions, and you'll encounter far fewer problems in the social media arena.

For all the potential disasters that exist within social media, there are an equal number of attributes. Thanks to the advent of social media, we can stay in touch with old friends and family, and we can even meet new friends and potential partners. Using questions in social media applies like it does in the "real world." We use questions to determine a person's thoughts, feelings, fears, and desires. "What is your favorite music?" can be a conversation starter online. So can "What did you study? How did that prepare you for the work you do now?"

Ultimately, the questions you ask the people you know are going to be different than those you ask the people you are just meeting. Like with the job, though, don't take questions for granted or expect you'll know a person's response because you've been friends for fifteen years. Quite often, you'll discover new aspects to your friends and family if you ask them open-ended questions about their lives, dreams, goals, and past.

Another important thing to remember online is the fact that subtlety, sarcasm, and irony can often be completely misread. It can be easy to misconstrue a person's comments and become infuriated when in reality they were making a harmless passing remark. One way to address this issue is to ask questions. Discern a person's meaning before you jump on that tirade. Give them a chance to explain. In terms of your own posts, comments, and online messages, be wary of vague statements or statements that may be perceived in a way they weren't intended. Remember the "Simple Rules of Communication"? They apply online as much as in-person! When we cannot discern the meaning of an individual by way of facial expression, it's all the more important to clarify our meaning.

**Consider the following questions to ask yourself before posting online:**

- What is my intention? What do I want to achieve by posting this comment, emailing this message, or sending this text?

- Is my intention clear? Or, is it possible this might be misinterpreted? If so, how do I rephrase the statement or question so that my intention is clear?

- Are there emoticons required? If you have to rely on a "winky-face" to ensure that the person you're addressing knows you're being snarky or sarcastic, consider how you might achieve that same intention without the emoticon. Can I say this differently so that they understand I'm joking? I'm not saying emoticons are always a no-no; but if we can learn to communicate without them, we're one step ahead in our goal of clear, simple communication.

- How will this make ___ feel? Are you posting drunken party photos of your friends? How would they feel about that? Are you discussing a major decision that someone is facing? How will your comment make them feel? Remember to examine how your posts and messages will affect others both emotionally and physically. Always ask yourself "How would I feel if ___ posted this?" Empathy is the ability to put yourself in someone else's shoes. Learning to ask yourself how your actions or comments will affect others will make you a more empathetic and conscientious friend.

- Am I listening? Are you taking in what the other person is saying, whether they are communicating on Facebook, by text message, or on the telephone? Do you truly understand their meaning? If not, ask them to clarify. "What do you mean by that?" "Are you saying ___?" Clarifying the statements and questions of others puts us that much closer to effectively connecting with them.

Just like in the workplace, communication via social media, email, text-message, and telephone is important. Knowing the potential elements of miscommunication is important as well. Always ensure that you're being clear by asking yourself "If I were ___, how would I respond to this?" And remember, just because social media is dominated by "statements," there is no reason that you can't use questions through modern communication methods in order to deepen and intensify your connections with your friends, family, and loved ones. You might be surprised at how much you can learn about the people you thought you knew.

## Online Dating – Segue to Sex, or Meeting Mister Right?

Although "online dating" is a relatively new invention, the concept has existed for many years. Before the internet, the process of finding a life partner through mass marketing dates back centuries. In the United States alone, the process of "advertising for a spouse" became widely popular with the expansion of the West. Because conditions were so harsh and the mortality rate so low, it was common to lose a wife in childbirth or a husband to overwork. Thus, novels like *Sarah, Plain and Tall* are not as absurd as one might think: with a population expanding into rural regions and often with miles in-between, the prospect of finding a wife down at the town market was minimal. Widows and widowers alike would post advertisements in regional or national papers to solicit correspondence and, if luck prevailed, a mate.

We'd like to think we've come so far, but in reality the reasons behind online dating today aren't that different than "personals ads" were 150 years ago. In an isolated and isolating world, it can be difficult to encounter "the one" from our day-to-day lives. You might be avoiding the potential catastrophe of dating someone from your office; you might spend so much time working that you don't have time to dally at clubs trying to pick up a mate; you might prefer the types of men or women that you wouldn't find in the common social arena – whatever your reasons for choosing to find a partner online, there are millions of others who agree.

According to "Online Dating Statistics 2012" on ansonalex.com, "The online dating industry has gone from a $900 million industry in 2007 to a $1.9 billion industry in 2012." Why? A major business doesn't thrive unless there's a driving demand for it. How effective are these dating sites? According to the same article,

"Since 2006, about 17% of married couples have met by using an online dating site." Not terrible odds.

## Making the First Move: What Questions Do I Ask?

The online dating arena is established around questions. Sites like okcupid.com specialize in developing a series of different surveys and questionnaires to determine the compatibility of its clients. Many other sites do the same. But what about after you've filled out the forms? How do you pose questions that aren't cliché to someone who might interest you? Below are several "starter" questions that can get a conversation going. Just like going into a job interview, consider what your objectives are: What are the important aspects of a romantic partner to you? How important is a potential date's career choices? Would you prefer being with someone who is divorced or never been married? Why?

Taking these questions into account will help you determine what's important and what questions to ask of your potential date. In the online dating world, we don't have the benefit of knowing about someone before we begin dating them – which is both an asset and a detriment. It is an asset because it leaves the playing field for questions wide open. It is a detriment at times because we cannot predetermine whether we will have that all-elusive "chemistry" with them when we meet face-to-face.

Once you've considered the important factors of a relationship and partner, your questions should be right in front of you. Open-ended questions will give you the most information about a person and allow for greater connection. Consider some of the following:

- Where are you from? Where did you grow up?

- What was your family like? Do you have siblings? How close are you?

- What do you think is important in a relationship?

- How long have you been on [X Dating Site]? What were your goals when you joined? Do you feel like it's been a good experience? Why?

- What are you passionate about? Why?

- What did you study? How did that contribute to your career/life?

- What do you enjoy doing for fun?

- What was your last relationship like?

# Self Communication – Asking the Hard Questions

We've discussed the importance of asking yourself questions before communicating with others and establishing your objective. In this chapter, we're going to look at those *questions that you should ask yourself* in order to determine your long-term objectives, short-term objectives, and actions.

## Determining Your Short-Term and Long-Term Objectives

Long-term objectives are what you want out of life *as a whole*. These objectives relate to those "monumental decisions" like who you want to spend your life with, what kind of career you choose, where you want to live, and how you want to spend the majority of your time. Surprisingly, many of us discover that we *thought* we knew the answers to these questions only to discover somewhere along the way that our answers have changed. That's why it's important to revisit them from time to time – both to remind ourselves of what we wanted previously and to assess if we still want the same things.

When our long-term objectives change, we should examine why they've changed and how we must change our actions accordingly. Consider the following questions to determine your long-term objectives in life. These are just a few of the "big" questions it's important to ask yourself as you begin to evaluate your life-plan:

- What am I the most passionate about? Why?

- What do I want in a relationship with a long-term partner? Why are these qualities important to me?

- What kind of job do I want? Why? What fulfills me about this profession?

- What is the most fulfilling thing I have achieved thus far in life? Why do I find that experience fulfilling?

- What excites me the most in my life? Why?

- Who do I enjoy spending time with? Why do I enjoy the company of these individuals?

- Where feels the most like "home" to me? Why?

- Where would I most like to live? Why?

- What does "family" mean to me? How do I want my own "family" to look?

- What are the most important aspects of friendship to me?

- How do I want to be perceived by others?

- What kind of work environment is the most satisfying to me? Why?

- How do I want to be remembered when I'm gone?

As we progress through life, we'll face an endless number of obstacles standing in our way. Remembering "why" we're pursuing what we're pursuing can lead us back on track toward our long-term objectives. Short-term objectives are the simpler steps that lead up to our long-term objectives. They often answer the question: "How?" "How do I go about pursuing a career in medicine?" "How do I meet Mr. Right?" "How do I find a place that feels like home?"

The answer to these questions will point you in the direction of your short-term objectives. "How do I go about pursuing a career in medicine?" will have different steps to reach the end result. Your first step might be "How do I determine the best place to study?" or "What area of specialization excites me the most?" Answering those questions will ultimately lead you closer to your objective of pursuing a career in medicine. Questions will lead your path in life if you allow them to. Questions can open your mind to an endless number of possibilities when you ask them of yourself, of those you love, and even of those you disagree with.

Understanding our objectives is the first step in formulating our questions. Why are you asking? What will you do with the answer? How will you proceed from here? Answer these questions in any situation and then remember to be direct, simple, and brief, maintain focus and intent, and listen!

> "Have patience with everything unresolved in your heart and to try to love the questions themselves as if they were locked rooms or books written in a very foreign language. Don't search for the answers, which could not be given to you now, because you would not be able to live them. And the point is to live everything. Live the questions now. Perhaps then, someday far in the future, you will gradually, without even noticing it, live your way into the answer." – Rainer Maria Rilke

## **Conclusion**

Knowing how to ask questions and which ones to ask in the right situations puts us a step ahead in the game. Questions can lead us to deeper personal connections with those we love and they can also lead us to greater success in the workplace. Understanding our objectives helps us to develop questions that provoke, engage, charm, and entice.

In this book, we've looked at a number of different questions within a variety of situations. The first consideration for each situation is "Why am I asking?" What do you want in terms of a response? Are you attempting to lead the other person into a particular frame of thought? Do you seek an elaborate answer or a direct answer? What are you trying to learn and why is it important? How does the information relate to your immediate and long-term objectives?

We've looked at different ways to use questions in order to open up an individual to sharing their thoughts, feelings, and desires. We've also looked at questions geared to establish trust, to illustrate learning, to guide, to inspire, and to enlighten. In this final section, we'll take a look at more questions to store in your reservoir. Consider these questions for yourself, for others, and in a variety of different situations. How could each of these questions be used to fulfill your own obstacles in life? Questions are the key to learning and the key to your success!

**More Questions to Consider**

- When did you first become inspired to pursue this career? What inspired you?

- Where would you like to see yourself in five years? In twenty?

- How do you want to be remembered?

- Who do you love the most? What do you love about this person?

- What is the most meaningful thing you have ever accomplished? Why was it meaningful to you?

- What do you think the world needs more of? What do you think the world needs less of? Why?

- What are your greatest regrets? What did you learn from these experiences?

- What would you like to improve about yourself? Why?

- If you found out you were going to die in one year, how would you spend that time? What would you do? Where would you go? What would to tell others?

- When is the most hurt you've ever felt? Why? What did you learn from this situation? How did this experience change the way you think and act?

- What qualities would you most like to instill in your children? Why are they important qualities to you?

- If money were no option, what would you choose to do with your life? What job would you have? How would you spend your time?

- What is the most meaningful thing anyone has ever said to you? Why was it meaningful?

- What do you fear the most? Why do you fear this? How reasonable is this fear?

- What are you the proudest of? Why are

you proud of this?

- How do you hope others feel about you? Why?

- What would you most like to give to the world?

Life is full of questions. When you ask one, you will find ten others behind it. Welcome them. Ask them of yourself and of others. Listen to the responses you hear, and examine them. Sometimes the answers you hear will surprise you – but those are moments to cherish. Learning about ourselves and others is how we grow and connect in this life. Cherish learning, cherish questions, cherish others – and you too will be cherished.

**Visit
EmpowermentNation.com
to view other fantastic books,
sign up for book alerts, giveaways,
and updates!**

www.ingramcontent.com/pod-product-compliance
Lightning Source LLC
Chambersburg PA
CBHW051728170526
45167CB00002B/848